SNAILS

ARE JUST MY

SPEED!

A TOON BOOK BY

KEVIN McCLOSKEY

For Brian, my youngest brother and oldest friend.

Editorial Director & Designer: FRANÇOISE MOULY

Guest Editor: RICHARD KUTNER

KEVIN McCLOSKEY'S artwork was painted with acrylic paint on parchment-style

SNAILS BUILD ROADS OF SLIMY MUCUS.

AMAZING SNAILS LIVE EVERYWHERE
ON EARTH: AT THE BOTTOM
OF THE SEA...

AND HIGH
UP IN THE
MOUNTAINS.

THERE ARE
HAIRY SNAILS
IN THE
RAIN
FOREST.

GLASS
SNAILS
HAVE A
SEE-
THROUGH
SHELL.

THE GIANT AFRICAN SNAIL*
CAN GROW TO 15 INCHES LONG.

* ALSO CALLED
THE TIGER SNAIL
BECAUSE OF ITS
STRIPES

THE ACMELLA
NANA SNAIL
IS SO SMALL
IT FITS
THROUGH
THE EYE
OF
A NEEDLE.

A SNAIL'S TONGUE CAN HAVE OVER 14,000 TEETH!

IT'S LIKE A GRATER OR A FILE.

EVEN THE COMMON GARDEN SNAIL IS AMAZING.

MAP of a SNAIL

- liver
- kidney
- lung
- stomach
- digestive gland
- heart
- dart sac
- foot
- mucus gland
- crop
- brain
- breathing pore
- eyes
- tentacle
- mouth
- tongue and teeth

A SNAIL'S EYES ARE WEAK, BUT IT USES ITS LOWER TENTACLES TO FEEL AND SMELL.

THERE ARE THOUSANDS OF KINDS OF SNAILS AND MANY MORE TYPES OF SLUGS. SLUGS ARE SNAILS WITHOUT SHELLS.

THE STORY OF CUPID'S ARROWS MAY HAVE COME FROM SNAILS' "LOVE DARTS."

...SNAILS ARE FUN TO DRAW!

Start with a 6.

Circle around a few times.

Close up the shell.

Draw the body and eyes.

Don't forget the mucus!

The trick with snails is to draw...

S-L-O-W-L-Y!

Lovely!

ABOUT THE AUTHOR

KEVIN McCLOSKEY teaches illustration at Pennsylvania's Kutztown University. After writing this book, Kevin is practically a snail expert, but he can't tell us whether the snails served in restaurants are tasty – he's never eaten one. What's the closest he's come to trying snails? Kevin says, "Sometimes, when I cook artichokes, I put a clove of garlic in the leaves. Then when they're cooked, I forget I put the garlic in and I think there's a slug in my food."

HOW TO READ COMICS WITH KIDS

Kids love comics! They are naturally drawn to the details in the pictures, which make them want to read the words. Comics beg for repeated readings and let both emerging and reluctant readers enjoy complex stories with a rich vocabulary. But since comics have their own grammar, here are a few tips for reading them with kids:

GUIDE YOUNG READERS: Use your finger to show your place in the text, but keep it at the bottom of the speaking character so it doesn't hide the very important facial expressions.

HAM IT UP! Think of the comic book story as a play and don't hesitate to read with expression and intonation. Assign parts or get kids to supply the sound effects, a great way to reinforce phonics skills.

LET THEM GUESS. Comics provide lots of context for the words, so emerging readers can make informed guesses. Like jigsaw puzzles, comics ask readers to make connections, so check a young audience's understanding by asking "What's this character thinking?" (but don't be surprised if a kid finds some of the comics' subtle details faster than you).

TALK ABOUT THE PICTURES. Point out how the artist paces the story with pauses (silent panels) or speeded-up action (a burst of short panels). Discuss how the size and shape of the panels carry meaning.

ABOVE ALL, ENJOY! There is of course never one right way to read, so go for the shared pleasure. Once children make the story happen in their imagination, they have discovered the thrill of reading, and you won't be able to stop them. At that point, just go get them more books, and more comics.

www.TOON-BOOKS.com

SEE OUR FREE ONLINE CARTOON MAKERS, LESSON PLANS, AND MUCH MORE